For Jim:

in gratitude
& delight
in our work together.

Fred Morlet

7/57

The First Place

Poetry U.S.A.

FRED MARCHANT

HOUSE ON WATER, HOUSE IN AIR

The Dedalus Press

HOUSE ON WATER, HOUSE ON AIR

poems by

Fred Marchant

Fred Marchant [signature]

DEDALUS

Dedalus, Dublin 2002

The Dedalus Press
24 The Heath ~ Cypress Downs ~ Dublin 6W
Ireland

ISBN 1 901233 87 1

The Dedalus Press gratefully acknowledges permission to reprint poems from Marchant's Word Works Washington Prize book *Tipping Point* [www.wordworksdc.com] and poems from *Full Moon Boat* published by Graywolf Press, Saint Paul, Minnesota, U.S.A. [www.graywolfpress.org]. Lists of the poems in these collections are given on the contents page.

Dedalus Press books are represented and distributed in the in the UK by **Central Books**, 99 Wallis Road, London E9 5LN

The Dedalus Press receives financial assistance from
An Chomhairle Ealaíon, The Arts Council, Ireland.

Printed in Dublin by Johnswood Press

Contents

New Poems

for Stefi

FROM *TIPPING POINT*

Published 1994 by

THE WORD WORKS, WASHINGTON DC

DIRECTIONS DOWN

First, you will have to cross
a talus slope, stretches of
sphagnum and low growth fern,
a purple cluster of lupine.

Then down through the dwarfed
evergreens, moss-shrouded,
miraculous to the touch,
the bark smooth as new flesh.

Hold onto whatever offers itself.
Be thankful for the roots rising
like knuckles and fists, and
for the deadfall which will stop

you should you trip. You might
feel the impulse to linger awhile,
maybe to listen to the wood thrush,
but the light will be dimming,

and there will be the knife-
edge, the sheer drop, the stones
unwilling to stand still and
pass you on gently to the next.

When you smell our cooking fires
and hear our prayers mingling,
we will know you are near.
We may be feeling ashamed

of the flaws you will find in us,
of the mistakes we have made,
of the crude place we have built
for you to live among us.

But we are part of who you are,
and we have been waiting a long time.
We are glad now to see you.
Oh, angel, landed, stay.

THE FOOT OF THE MOUNTAIN

Before I learned to speak
I knew what my father's hand
sounded like when it struck
my mother on the face.

I could tell from afar
and from under the pillow
the difference between
an open palm and the fist.

Slap was precise, pointed,
and lightning clear.
Afterward, the air was almost
sweet with particles of relief.

Punch — strange, goofy
word — was a furtive,
inward-looking sound,
as if it hoped it had not been heard.

Curses too sounded like slap
and punch. "Bastard"
clattered through the air.
"Sonofabitch," however,

sucked the breath out.
I had no idea of meaning,
but rather, the tones I heard
were the pure being of these.

Now my father can hardly speak.
His lungs move only enough air
across his cords to whisper,
or whistle involuntarily.

Maybe he wants to say,
"Forgive me," but always
there had been nothing
but a steep granite silence

between us, and it is now
all the more brilliant
and uninviting in the clear
blue light at the top.

MAGNIFICATION

Roseate spoonbills — shy, retreating
into the mangrove. The guidebook
says the species has been battered
and does not trust us. I stand at the rail
overlooking the pan-flat, tidal swamp,
adjusting the field glasses, my eyes
training on the mostly still, nearly
camouflaged smudges of pink.

In my tightened breathing, in the light
through the vines in the distant hollow
I see a moment of my own waking —
me a first-grader on a long oak bench,
my mother and I waiting for a train,
the sunlight marching through wired,
cathedral windows, and dust floating,
upheld in the beams, the pigeons cooing.

My mother's cheek bruised blue-green.
A welt high on her nose where her
glasses pressed. This was flight,
her intended escape down the Eastern
seaboard. I was deep in my bright
comic, one of the *Tales of the Unknown*,
and nibbling from my stash a crumbly,
cheese-flavoured, peanut-butter cracker.

Suddenly a whistle bored in, the marble
floor shuddered, and the *Minuteman's* bell
sounded frantic, mad. Overhead, a voice
announced, magnified, and distorted
the names of what lay before us.
Pigeons leapt into the lime-streaked vault.
We gathered together what we had
and took our two places in the line.

BORAXO

He would flick his middle finger at the tin,
    and sprinkle out a mound
        of stark, alkaline powder.

Cupping it in his palm, he would begin
    an almost punitive scrub:
        knuckles, wrists, elbows;

rinse, scan for the hidden grease,
    and start again, the soap
        floating an oily, fish-grey skim.

At the table, beaming like a grandee,
    he would rub his palms
        together to hear the hiss

of his own clean dry flesh, and as he
    counted up the blessings:
        house, son, wife,

he would hold his hands out for us to see,
    declaring, "Now this,
        this is the life."

VIETNAM ERA

In 1959 you were thirteen and rose
    earlier than you ever
imagined, knowing birds had nothing
    on you, leaving
on an empty stomach to deliver the news,
    ignoring your mother's
sleepy warnings, beating your lathered
    father out the door,
to hop now on the company bike
    and ride to the station
where your *Globes* and *Heralds* waited
    to be folded and stuffed
into the wire basket, the canvas bag.
    Let everyone else go
fishing: you patrolled an uncharted
    city, a zone dawning
in headlines and traffic. You were
    losing baby fat and
saving money for school. The papers
    you heaved you imagined
grenades, and that the porches they
    landed on burst into flame,
sending the little girls out flying
    straight into your arms,
arms already smeared with the ink
    from the world's bloody
deeds, your own war only seven years away.

ELEPHANTS WALKING

Curled in a window seat, level with wind-swayed oak,
    aching on a green vinyl pad,
I think of the fortunes spent on the hardwood, wainscot
    study, and the slates fitted
for the arbour walkways, the labour it took to lug bricks out
    to each overly articulated
corner, in which nook a child of fortune, cushion-tassel
    between his fingers, might
look up from his reading to see in the heat waves rising
    over the pale, shimmering
delphinium, a plot miracle perhaps, the strange death
    by spontaneous combustion
in *Our Mutual Friend*, and the child wondering how, why,
    and could it have been?

My childhood bedroom, summer night, one hand marking
    the book, the other's palm
and fingers printing moist, disappearing shadows on the wall.
    Then the college library,
Harkness Hall, and aged, white-cowled Father Benilde
    smelling of coffee, muscatel,
and Old Spice as he opened the doors at 7:30. First in line,
    I was all business, heading
straight to my end of the long, immovable table, to my first
    reading of Dante, a paperback
copy of Ciardi, with its cover of red, grinning, cartoon
    devils, which I had in a fit
of verisimilitude (a word I had just learned)
    charred with a lighter.

My first lines that year: "Butt, butt, base, bale beast.
        I fear your horns not
in the least!" The intended tone was courtly love,
        but the words were
apostrophe to a buffalo in Roger Williams Park,
        one that had leaned
hard into the sagging hurricane fence near my date.
        The lines came to me
as I woke after a nap in the library. I still love
        to sleep in libraries
whenever I can. I fix my head sideways over
        my folded hands,
and make room for the little puddle of drool
        I'll quickly wipe away.
I wake into a barely believable clarity
        throughout my body.
I'm ready to grapple with fate, love, sex,
        the stirrings within.
Over readers and sleepers alike hovers a mist
        or a pollen, and in it
I see words shuttling back and forth like birds.
        In the darkness or dream
something hugely important has been free
        to roam. Grateful,
I say to myself, "Elephants have been walking."

"Son, we must give this country great poetry!"
        decreed the older poet
to my nodding head, as he shook my hand after
        the Crystal Room reading.

Later, as I walked back to my dormitory, sleet
        failing to cool me
I turned his pronoun over and over, thinking
        yes, we do, *we* do.
On the news there was the familiar footage:
        a Phantom run
ending in a hypnotic burst of lit yellow napalm.
        I knew the war
was wrong, but that was why, I claimed, I should go,
        to sing the song
of high lament, to get it into the books. Like Ishmael
        I would sign on
for a three-year voyage under a madman captain.
        Frissons to be had
instantly: a pity-the-youth-soon-dying look in the eyes.
        "Are you crazy?"
asked my girlfriend. But I was filled with vibrant life
        and felt neither suicidal
nor confused when I dialled the Marine recruiter: "Yes,
        I look forward to reporting."
Phone in my lap, I sat sideways, my legs dangling
        over the arms of my red
leather reading chair. A warm spring wind was
        melting the snow
down to bright medallions of ice. I felt clear-headed
        and refreshed.
I just hoped the war would last until I got there.
        Elephants were walking.

MALEBOLGE

Okinawa, 1970

The Bachelor Officer's Quarters. 'A Sunday morning,
    my eyes drifting vaguely
over the gypsum ceiling tiles, and over cinder blocks
    as desolate as craters.
Outside the sugar cane hisses, palm fronds clack,
    and a rainstorm darkens
a quadrant of sunlight. Next door, the junior supply
    officer has begun to stir
under his cadre of taped-up Playmates smiling down,
    an air-brushed, backlit
canopy for the boy pasha. In my room, hands behind
    my head, I am deciding
to quit the Marine Corps as a conscientious objector.

Nei-San is how it might be spelled phonetically.
    Sister or *Miss*
in Japanese, but we use it for the Okinawan maids.
    My roommate has
what is called a "ranch" and spends his weekends
    with our *Nei-San*
in a house outside the gate. How easily we all take
    to the minor pleasures
of empire: *Nei-Sans* to brasso our belt buckles, to wash
    and starch our uniforms,
to spit-polish our boots. Our presence helps, we are told,
    "the local economy."

In the morning when we leave for our work, the *Nei-Sans*
    are setting up, squatting
near the soapy showers, their hot-plates lit, tea-water
    simmering, and Ryukyuan
radio music tuned in. A hard, flattening light pours in
    onto a faded tatami.
I want to linger behind and listen to their jokes about us,
    the young lieutenant-sans.

In Book VI of the *Iliad*, Adrestos falls to Menelaos.
    Wrapping his arms
around the wronged king's knees, Adrestos begs for his life,
    and Menelaos wavers . . .
but as the gods would have it, Agamemnon discovers them
    and rebukes his brother
for softness bordering on the feminine. Then he spears
    Adrestos in the belly,
and as he withdraws the blade, sets his foot on the man's
    ribs for leverage,
saying not even children in the womb are to be spared.
    I dream I am under arms,
helmeted in bronze, with a raised horsehair plume.
    My enemy wrestles me
into submission, and I bite him full on the calf.
    His blood wells up
like a spring, tasting like smoke and quicksilver.
    I sip it and do not die.

The strangest moment in the *Inferno*: when Dante's arms
     are wrapped around
the shoulders of Virgil, who is himself climbing down
     the coarse-haired flank
of Satan, whose enormous body is locked in a lake of ice.
     Suddenly Virgil seems
to be climbing back up, and Dante is bewildered,
     terrified as a child,
and needs to be told they have just passed through
     the core of the fallen
world and they are now hand over hand on their way
     to the earth's other side.

In Tengan, in Camp Smedley T. Butler, named after
     a general who in disgust
at the "banana wars" turned in his medals and quit;
     on a thickly flowered,
half-jungle hillside overlooking the Brig and a sea
     of sugar cane the escapees
loved like life itself; in a white blockhouse, on a spartan
     single bed, in skivvies
and flip-flops, I ask myself again what *would* I
     be willing to trade,
what part of my body, how much of my life would I pay
     for one poem, one true
line about this war. Then a voice not quite my own,
     but close to my face
and as if behind a wire mesh wonders just how grand,
     how filled with epiphany
the poem would have to be if the cost was an arm or more
     belonging to another?

Ganesh, son of Shiva and Parvati, has a pot-bellied
        human torso and an
elephant's head. Beloved by all, he blesses beginnings:
        businesses, marriages,
births. He is also the patron of writers, an inspirer
        of epic poems.
He might as a series of small tremors step through me
        when he rises out
of the cane fields into clouds swollen with rainwater
        from the east.
I wish I could seek his protection in the months it will
        take me to get out.
He would set my penance at twenty years of silence,
        my words curling up
like leaves and blowing away. But even if this were so,
        I would still claim
the quick, half-audible "no" I said out loud was mine.

TIPPING POINT

Late blue light, the East
      China Sea, a half-mile out . . .
            masked, snorkelled, finned,

rising for air, longing for it,
      and in love with the green
            knife-edged hillsides, the thick

aromatic forests, and not ready
      for the line of B-52's coming in
            low on the horizon, three airplanes

at a time, bomb-empty after
      the all-day run to Vietnam.
            Long, shuddering wings, and predatory,

dorsal tail-fins, underbelly
      in white camouflage, the rest
            jungle-green, saural, as if a gecko had

grown wings, a tail-fin, and
      nightmare proportions. Chest deep,
            on the reef-edge, I think of the war smell

which makes it back here:
      damp red clay, cordite, and fear-salts
            woven into the fabric of everything not

metal: tarps, webbed belts,
      and especially jungle "utes,"
            the utilities, the fatigue blouses

and trousers which were not
       supposed to rip, but breathe,
              and breathe they do — not so much

of death — but rather the long
       living with it, sleeping in it,
              not ever washing your body free of it.

A corporal asked me if he still stank,
       I told him no, and he said,
              "With all due respect, Lieutenant,

I don't believe you." A sea snake,
       habu, slips among the corals,
              and I hover while it slowly passes.

My blue surf mat wraps its rope
       around me, tugs inland
              at my hips while I drift over ranges

of thick, branching elkhorn,
       over lilac-pale anemones,
              over the crown-of-thorns starfish,

and urchins spinier than naval
       mines, over mottled slugs,
              half-buried clams, iridescent angelfish.

The commanding general said,
       "Every man has a tipping point,
              a place where his principles give way."

I told him I did not *belong*
     to any nation on earth, but
          a chill shift of wind, its hint of squall

beyond the mountain tells me
     no matter what I said or how,
          it will be a long swim back,
               complicities in tow.

MAYAN FIGURES IN STONE

O we could be solemn and teach
you, or pretend
to teach you some lessons still

in what it means to worship and
be worshipped.
We could show you the sense

of heaving the body upward,
the purpose of
climbing in pursuit of the spirit.

We could show you holds in the living
rock, reveal
the corbel arches embedded in

the secret centre, the ceremonially
intended replica
of all the balanced forces locked

together in silicates of belief.
We could sweat
you through one human step after

another, parting the layers of heat,
pressing you
to us, letting you hear the thin, wet

chatter of limestone, the whispers
of quartz with
granite, the stone telling the truth

about sacrifice, how we delivered
ourselves freely,
releasing our hopes like birds

we had taught never to return,
how we too
hovered, not ever wanting to die.

HERONS

In a grey curve of tidal flat,
scores of herons stock still,

heads cocked at oblique angles,
water ruffling at their legs.

The herring see only sets of yellow
weed-stems rising bolt upright.

They cannot imagine the orange,
unlidded eye of God, how poised

it is, how steady its aim.

WARTIME

The soul is always beautiful,
The universe is in order, everything is in its place.

Whitman, *The Sleepers*

i.

      Oranges, clementines, green daffodil stems, yellow
horns, good light. Our mahogany table.
           I wonder how many loaded bombers
                flew from Maine.
           I wonder what the ground trembling
                felt like within it.

      Here in Belmont, the paperboy rings our bell
saying he's got the flu,
           and could we call his Dad to take
                him home. It is wet,
January, but Dad does not thank me.
           He is disappointed in Mikey.

      One line that stays from the *Agamemnon* is about
the storm that brought
           the Argives home from Troy:
                "the sea bloomed with corpses."
           The way wildflowers in the
                desert overnight spring.

ii.

The première. Snow
    in oversized flakes.
        Predictions way too low.

In the room of negotiation
    ministers defter than ghosts
        touch for the cameras.

We joke, the student and I:
    he needs a design, a logo
        for the cover of his magazine.

I suggest *Death Before*
    Dishonour, in scrolled letters,
        heraldic, under crossed daggers,

or maybe it's only one,
    the memory is dim: blue
        and green lines of bright tattoo,

with red ink inserted
    under the skin and shaped
        to look like perfect drops.

"That's the one you want, right?"

iii.

Years ago in the deserts of Utah
    I would go days without words,

drugged with red rock, hiking in the Maze,
    relieved of my life, touching the rock wall,

a chipped Kokopelli flute, fingertips
    tracing the curved arch, the brittle spine.

Now this: printed on grainy manila,
    page three, an earnest, moonfaced G.I.

at the window of a burned-out truck,
    a corpse fried to the seat springs. Caption:

Iraqi Dead . . . No shit.
    The G.I.'s lips teeter on the edge of hilarity.

Thinks he's really seeing something.
    How solemn the shape, stretched and still.

Two of us: pausing, gazing, bending, stopping.

iv.

Like the commanders from their maps
I leave the television and take to bed
the play-symbol derricks, tanks, planes,
the corridors of regimentally shaded terrain.

Out of the white nub of the earphone
I siphon in the talk radio. *Traitor,*
a woman flings the word as if
it could flare in our common night.

When I wake, the *Quick, boys!*
of Owen's nightmare
circles over the low, undisturbed
places where the poison has settled.

In the morning paper's quippy
column I catch a whiff:
"As for the old conscientious objection . . .
better leave it off the resumé".

v.

On the television, the fishbone-lean little general who is fond
of the metaphor, "the fog of war". No one, he says, can see the
whole picture. No one knows what the other fellow is doing.
Sometimes, he says, it's not even clear to yourself what you are
doing.

I remember my first morning in the Marine Corps. Long be-
fore sunlight, we were outside standing at attention, eyes
locked straight ahead, feet at a forty-five degree angle, heels
touching, and soles on the painted footprints which told the
platoon how to form itself. The drill instructor announced that
on his command each of us would turn right and step off with
the left foot, and that thereafter the left foot would always be
striking the deck to the sound of *Laeouff*. The right foot, he
said, would be landing to the sound of *Heidle*. Strung together,
they composed a marching cadence which sounded like this:

Laeouff—heidle—laeouw—heidle—laeouw—heidle—louw
         . . . laeouff—heidl—louw
                 . . . laeouff—heidle—louw

Cadence, in other words, began with four beats, followed by a

pair of trimeter lines. Yet every drill instructor put a signature
on his cadence by cutting and twirling syllables like a scat
singer. Along with the feel of improvisation, there was a thread
of the joyful, as if the instructor were an outsized woodthrush
presiding over a scale that nature had allotted and commanded
him to sing. It was a beautiful sound floating over our heads
and governing, guiding us to the mess hall in the early morning
darkness.

Had I been asked that morning I would have said I understood
Billy Budd. I would have said it was a parable about how the
world cannot tolerate the persistently innocent. I would have
said it was the archetypal "inside narrative," about wars in the
soul, not wars of the European imperium. In pidgen, "Christ
and Billy, same-same."

Today, though, I think of the strangest moment in that story.
Just before Vere signals the hangman, Billy shouts without a
trace of the fatal stammer, "God bless Captain Vere." Despite
being appalled at what is happening to Billy, the crew repeats
his blessing in antiphonal response. Maybe they are being
ironic. Maybe they so love the Handsome Sailor they will re-
peat whatever he says. As Billy's body rises in the fleece-lined
dawn, the warship beneath them cuts through moderate seas, a
nation unto itself, ponderously cannoned.

vi.

A woman on the radio describing her mother's wounds:
World War 11, the Philippines, an airport strafing
left her with six scooped-out, star-shaped scars
on her back and thighs, each with a rough ridge
of flesh the child who then believed in the sweet,
oily powers of Jergens hoped she could make vanish

34

if only she worked the lotion in deeply enough.

These were wonders we had no
account whereof. Thus we questioned
the child vigorously . . .

How many times, she was asked, did you try this?

and in time
she admitted slipping through keyholes,
and had upon occasion been a cat,
a mare, a stoat.

War, she answered, disfigures everyone.

All matter is dead. We know this.

vii.

What is it then between us?

Is it a cold snap, the Square empty, a taxi breaking
from line and heading straight at me,
its wake whipping into chill benzene wind?

Is it the news-stand in silver light, tall glossies
declaring the war in thick, opulent letters,
announcing we are stoic and firm?

There is something in us that loves this.

It lances a pressure, leeches a poison,
shades the trivial in lurid colour: O sweet
portents, O death which helps us feel!

This is how our uneasiness works,
all our goods waving like the legumes
of the prairie under an utterly empty blue.

Imagine the pearly chenille on the bed,
the Smith & Wesson revolver oiled,
the polished holster glinting with prohibition,

the miraculous blue tint of the forging,
the sweet heft, the woodpanel grip,
almost human to the touch, notched.

Or think of your own foot hard on the accelerator,
eight lanes from Logan down to two in the tunnel,
and the fenders nosing near, *Fuck you!*

Or the subway roaring under the city on the hill,
the gold dome of the State House rising
like a mortar shell from its tube.

Step off the train and ride the escalator up,
into the cold snap, the Square,
the taxi heading straight for you.

Sometimes I think there's nothing left between us.
Not even words.

viii.

What was the state of your knowledge concerning
eternal life last spring?

I knew the spirits of the dead were around.
I believed, but did not know for certain,
that they inhabited the forms of the beautiful.

Please be more specific.

In certain slants of light, in sea-feathers
on a jetty, in the rustling of palms.
Perhaps there were others less congenial.

Did you recognise any?

Of course not. They were anonymous,
abstract. More like rhythms.
I gave them names of those I loved.

Go on.

I remember they were plentiful that year,
a swarming light and shadow play,
abundant, yet easy to ignore.

RESCUE

I wake and listen to a machine
growl through last night's snow,
and I remember trains coupling
in the railyard by the cemetery.

I remember being frightened,
calling out, my mother coming
to calm me and explain why
the work went on all night.

I also remember their sounds,
those I didn't dare ask about.
I would curl and recoil,
wall them out with my pillow.

Now the sound of whatever love
they had comes to me like a letter
I tear open with a pleasure
I never dreamed I would have.

I want to run into their room,
climb in under the covering years,
breathe in their strong night smell,
and tell them both they will not die.

HOSPITAL FOOD

After they bring the usual fare,
the canned wedges of peach,
the raspberry jello, the bland
concoctions of gravied meats,
the milk in waxy little cartons,
after all that for which I have
no stomach, my husband will
arrive with my robe and night-gown,
my rosary beads blessed by the Pope,
and my purse with the hidden check.
He will arrive under a cloud of
nervous energy, breath whiskied
and ripe, and as he unpacks the bag,
he will be saying, "Just a minute,
just a minute!" And I will feel again
his wish that I were already gone,
and his eyes when I meet them
will be as hateful to me as his words
about the need for a wheelchair,
or the danger of the rugs, and how
I cannot tie my own shoes. He will
say then he cannot understand
why I am crying, and I will tell him,
"I am not. I *am not!*"

Starlight Mints

i.

For months I have spoken on behalf of my aged
    and inarticulate father.
I try to be orderly describing his symptoms:

inner to outer, morning to night. Prostate cancer.
    Emphysema. Both
advanced. In the former, the home of maleness,

the fountain of youth, the spring of come,
    the walnut, however
you want it, has, in my father's own words,

"turned bad." In the other disease, the far reaches
    of his lungs have begun
to explode, tissue pulling itself apart, searching for

any pink remnant still capable of the oxygen
    exchange. Hunched
in the wheelchair beside me, the man is drowning.

ii.

I, 45, in perfect health, too fat for my own good,
    but filled with a sense
of lasting, the world of the body still mine, while his

world belongs to his memory and needs too much air
    for him to bother even
to recall. The contrast-gainer, I cannot help but dote

on the present tense of the bodies of passing nurses,
      their nylons whispering.
Discreet, attentive as a twelve-year-old to the shapes

under the underwear, to thin fabric, to bra-straps,
      to lips and nails brightened
by Eros, not the mighty, vehement god, but a daimon,

flickering in white light among the newly washed
      and the mostly well,
making me ache for the *little death*, its salt smell of youth.

iii.

Two years ago I peeked at his chart. The nurse said
      his body was "wasted."
He has lost a pound a month ever since. Eighty-five

is what he tips. His biceps are as thin as my wrists.
      His jade ring now spins
around the bone of his middle finger. His ribs tube

like a birdcage. When he walks he looks drunken,
      as if the planet wobbled
on its axis underneath him. He fidgets with a *People*,

then unwraps a Starlight Mint. The sound his mouth
      makes is not exactly
a smacking of his lips, but more a devoted sucking

that I can't stand to listen to. He is after little puffs
      of air over the candy.
"Try not to be so loud," I whisper, feeling better

that I have made my real wishes known to him,
        but then he forgets and I,
ill-tempered and embarrassed, need to tell him again.

iv.

What has passed between us in the forms of language
        has been plainer than
doorknobs. He is either "pretty good," or "not bad,"

or "no good," each of which might denote the identical
        condition. If he were God,
ours might be a world where language didn't matter.

Words for him were at best an affliction, bees
        suddenly infesting
the rotten eaves of a clapboard house. As a boy,

he stuttered, and I can only imagine the wrenching
        self-discipline it took him,
as he said, to straighten out. He used to shout at me,

"6-B! 6-B!" this, his coded complaint that at ten,
        with his father dead,
his mother had made him go to work pumping gas,

changing tires. The station a school where
        he learned the language
of practical men: fillerup, fin, *fucking engine!*

v.

Poet? Poetry? Could he have predicted a son like me?
    Once when I accused him
of not wanting to know what my life was really like,

he summoned a breath to say, "You'll never know
    how much". A sentence
with a sentence-sound, as Frost would have noted,

you had to reckon with, which is what I am doing
    when they call for us.
I wheel him in and help him stand. The nurse asks

how is he feeling. He steadies himself at the edge
    of the papered table,
his Jockeys down, baggy on his thighs. "Oooh Walter . . .

there's practically nothing left of you."

Nearly transparent flesh, pelvic blades, and pressed
    to his hip, the cellophane
wrap from a Starlight Mint. Not one of us says a word.

RED'S MEADOW
for W.L.M.

In the night, endless switchbacks, with pine
and fir leaning over smooth blacktop
and growing out of pale, pumice topsoil.
Morning: horse smell through the window,
sugar pines, scattered cones, larkspur, a stream.

When I called you, I shouted into the pay phone:
"A beautiful place, the middle of the mountains!"
I don't know what I expected you to say.
Later I heard you had cursed the nurse
for a pint she found hidden under a cushion.

Right before you died I too said no whiskey,
not on an empty stomach, yet I poured you
a shot anyway. You barely sipped it, but the smell
must have been like an old friend, a comfort.
Then you said, "I'm near the end."

I flinched and smiled and loved the way
the words thickened the minute, resisting
what hurried along. I should have pushed
back too when the intern used the word
"pretzel" as a verb to describe you folding

your legs up and in. I should have said,
even here among the machines mapping
the heart's long climb, its leap from range
to range, even here in these night mountains
is a meadow, *a lea, a place of light shining.*

FROM *FULL MOON BOAT*

Published 2000 by

GRAYWOLF PRESS

THE RETURN

When he poured acid for his etching,
Blake said the art he practised was infernal,
meaning it brimmed with the energy of demons
who first of all had been angels. On the wall
of the bedroom I inherited from my grandfather
hung a gold-framed etching titled "The Return" —
a doughboy kneeling before a larger-than-life
crucifix, the helmet and rifle on the floor,
his calves wrapped with puttees, his head
half-hidden by a bulging, cinched-up knapsack.

Harry, older uncle on my mother's side,
quit college to go to France in 1916.
He flew a Spad in the Lafayette Escadrille,
and never wanted to fly again afterwards.
In one photo the polished sash of his Sam
Browne belt gleams in the ocean sunlight.
He is sailing home, and a swell has leaned
him into the bulkhead. Under the smile
you can see his fear that life thereafter
would turn out to be another flying coffin.

In 1970, Georgette, Harry's war bride,
wrote to me on Okinawa, pleading that
I not leave the service as a conscientious
objector. She said Jesus could not approve,
He had smiled on America, and I owed
back some portion of what I had been given.

The airplane I flew home on, my c.o.
discharge in hand, was an empty, airborne
auditorium, another sign of the nation's excesses.
When I woke, I looked out over the desert,

and at first I thought I saw a land split
apart by our history of rage and sorrow,
but as we cruised through a vast clarity
of air thousands of feet up, the creases
of deep, dried-out arroyos reminded me
of the pack that belonged to the soldier
who hung over my childhood sleep
and taught me, before I ever understood
a word like *puttee*, how good it would feel
to take a helmet off, set the weapon down.

WAX

My mother coming to me, trying to comfort.
But am I the child crying? Is she coming *for*?

Her terrible fearsweat.

A moat of summer night, circle of innocence,
All the world's windows wide open, crying.

All ears, I,

And sanctuary while a car, whose headlights swing
Across the room, stops, idles.

She is crying.

All ears the maples and elms, the pointy leaves sifting her whispers.
And then me too.

Me too in the afterstorm,

"Don't worry," I say, but we worry,
We worry like candles wavering, alert, spilling,

All the long blue night.

OCTANE

I began in the realm of engine
and lit workbench, down among
unsorted screws, nuts, and washers,
next to a monkey wrench and ballpeen
hammer, with ratchets, and a vise grip,
its teeth broken, the bar shiny from use.
I climbed among black horns of radiator
hoses, and poked at discard batteries,
their acids bubbling from within.
I stood at attention by lit-up pumps,
those idols draped with red, plastic
pennants. Probed the iridescent gobs
of grease, breathed in a vivid, wavering
gasoline that wanted only a match,
longed to be radically other,
to be a flare of pure becoming, so bright
no one would know who else had been there,
whose hands had held and lifted me up.

THE FROG

Ciborium—nuns—broad breastplates of starched radiance—
a soupspill at lunch—an orange dot of need—my desire
to touch—the crisp cloth would hum like a tuning fork—
the frog—hidden in a fold—a clicker painted green—
metal flap for the belly—one click to stand—two to sit—
oaken pews smoothed by the spines curved into them—
tingly sweetness of incense—the priest's arms uplifted
and roping the light—the Paschal candle tall as a man—
creamy yellow—wax pooling and ready to spill—three clicks—
cool in the dark—we alcoved lambs—high heels tapping
to the rail—worn heels—seamed nylon calves—wrinkles on
the cloth—the body imposed, imposing—always the bottom—
the underneath, the creases—a nun who swirled in silence—
cat's-paw crepe of her soles—four clicks—at the left ear—
the light of the world—on my knees again.

DIANA'S LAMP

An ivory slide rule left me by my grandfather
became a measuring wand, my prophet and sign
of bent-over-a-hairline calibrations of the real.

He was waked in the living room. A priest
intoned a full rosary above him, and I was told
to stay put on the velvet chair, to be quiet

under a lamp made out of a cast of the goddess,
her bow in hand, a quiver of arrows on her back,
one breast out of her tunic. Trailed by whippets,

she walked under a curling brass vine, at the tip
of which was a bulb that shone with the same
thin light that falls now on the white pines

outside my window, and on the cords of cut timber
thickened by imagined elements of earth and heaven,
neither of which is the nature I long for anymore.

AFRICAN VIOLETS

In the empty part of the afternoon,
      perhaps the hour between two and three,
a time when you sneak a nap,
when a deliveryman pulls his truck under a tree
      certain no one would know the difference.
For my mother it would be just before that driver
      got home, when there would be a time she would
        call free, and mean free enough to pour out
her suffering and worry.

How I hated to have to listen.
How I listened as hard as I could.
It was like having a constant sunburn, with her hand
      resting on it.

Betrayal, beatings, an abandonment,
      the nightly tray with whiskey and beer
my father carried up to his mother in our attic flat.
When he came down to eat his supper,
      he would be ready to fight. His mother would have said
        his wife needed "a talking to."
There would be bruises, a broken pair of glasses,
      and all the next day tears that seemed to ooze.

Here is the lesson about the nature of love:
      never swear at a woman, never raise my hand.
I don't remember what I said in return,
      I said so little.
I was pure listening in training,
I sat as far away from her as I could,
      the far end of the couch, and across the room
where a blond throw rug from China was between us.

It was next to the table with African violets,
        where I studied their leaves, deep purple petals,
            and bright yellow eyes at the heart.

It would be this time of day,
        when lemon-yellow light warms the rug
and feeds the indoor flowers that quiver whenever
        a car slows and sounds as if it will stop.
An hour when people who know each other
        better than they know themselves
murmur words that are truer in tone than meaning.

When simplicities of feeling are offered as promises,
        gifts are accepted, and lessons learned,
            no matter how much they hurt.

THE PALE

You want to give me credit for being
unlike where we came from, neither
planed nor patted down. . .

but I, standing in front of your students
try to explain. My mother was divorced
and remarried, and thus

excommunicated, "denied the sacraments."
This made me, spiritually, a parish ward,
"a little bastard,"

according to the pious Father Prime,
who said it was a good lesson to learn
about the nature of sin.

So it was not the same as with you,
not skin colour, but more an eddy of barely
perceptible distress,

which swirled round us whenever we knelt,
palms together, tongues lifted, eyes shut,
elbows on the rail.

I remember our blue ties askew,
our shirttails wandering up from our belts,
and both of us somehow already beyond.

PROVIDENCE, HALFWAY

I'd like to wake at sea, rise at dawn and paint
the disappearing night fog — shades of white
for the fog, shades of black for the rest.

I would resist thinking these had anything to do
with race, or the memory of a morning centered
on me and Eddie Bolden, on different sides

of a rusted fence, him black, me white, and neither
of us much beyond six, grasses up to our thighs,
as we spoke about what I cannot recall,

but am certain was not a reason to punch me
in the face, which he wound up and did anyway.
Was I bragging about my clothes, the yard?

Or was it a tone that he alone could hear,
one that said I thought the world was good,
or would be, at least to me. Something about

my easy smile under fair-weather clouds
and shade catalpas where neighbourhoods
abutted, the corner of Camp Street and Locust,

halfway up the hill to Hope and some other
names for irony that have washed ashore
here in Providence and its adjacent Plantations.

THIRTY OBLIGATORY BOWS

Television last night,
a smooth homage to Hotel Company, bleeding on Hill 881.
The remembered command to a private to retrieve another,
then two of them dead. The former lieutenant,

his high-pitched voice, his almost-tears,
the "human interest" in those tears, the announcer pausing.
My skin crawling in the easy chair.
A flying reel of relived arguments, distinctions,

then the spool out of control, film flapping away.
The lieutenant reporting he was spit on.
My wondering if I had to believe him.
My feeling mean-spirited at my wondering.

He owns the largest garden centre in L.A.,
all that life under translucent plastic tenting,
From the steps of the pagoda where Thich Quang Duc
left to burn himself in Saigon, I took a photograph

which centered on a dragon boat
drifting on the Perfume River, framed by a full-leafed
banana tree. An image of mourning.
Another photograph: this one in front of the Marine insignia,

my right hand raised, joining. I am flanked
by my parents, their eyes odd and empty too.
It was 1968, and none of us knew what we were doing.
Upstairs, over my desk hangs a plaque with horns

from a Vietnamese mountain deer.
At school I have a lacquer of a poet wearing spectacles,
squatting, writing with a brush.
He lives near the One Pillar Pagoda.

My shelves are crowded with the books I teach:
the anatomies of sorrow, almanacs and unit histories,
Time-Life photo collections, topographical maps,
all the explanations I will ever need.

Today my friend To Nhuan Vy
and his young daughter Dieu Linh are coming to visit.
She has never seen snow before, and kneels down,
touches it to her face, is surprised and delighted.

Now they are on the salted steps and I shout out
Be careful, it's very slippery here!
The words float in the freezing air. Thirty years since,
and everything's changed, but not utterly.

ARCHIVES

The photographs are kept in flint-grey boxes,
wheeled in on waist-high carts that squeak
and irritate the researcher taking notes nearby.
I lift the flimsy, protective tissue as if it were
gauze through which blood has been seeping,
and beneath is a field hospital where a medic
tends to a civilian woman's wounded hip.
His eyes say she's worse off than she thinks.

Next is a corpse in a hammering sun, torso
twisted over his legs. Squatting beside him
is a boy whose bare white arms rest lightly
on his knees, a cigarette in his cupped hand.
The asked-for smile floats on his face,
is embarrassed and loyal only to the dead.

BONES TO HANOI

He is wary in the train station,
the rucksack bundled in his arms
as if it were holy. He tries to be
casual so as not to let anyone think
it is important enough to steal.
There is a policy which forbids
boarding a train with the remains
of a body, but surely others have
done so, even if the train would
then be haunted by an unburied
soul, and dangerous for a while.
But these are a brother's bones,
coming back from a ditch in
the South. Ten years and still
many are intact. Tibia, fibula,
digits, vertebrae. How can he
be sure he has them all or whose
are which? Pieces are scattered
at the bottom of the rucksack,
inside the curve of half-ribs
that fence his toiletries, a change
of clothing. Such packing makes
it very difficult to find his novel,
so he sits like a peasant to market,
leaning on what no one knows
he holds. He feels devoid of
thoughts other than suspicion,
and feels dry-hardened as these
he loves, carries, and cannot smell.

INSCRIPTION

People ask you for lullabies.
They want you to blow dust off the roses.
They'll tell you your job is to imagine engines have hearts.
I think it is best to say nothing.
Tell it to no one. Be armour and sloth.
Tell them there is nothing more to be said.
Let them think you are dead.

DELPHI

i.

"I" —
the very use of that pronoun was what I had come to suspect.
I said, "Because being is but a solvent,
the ego is not separate from space or time, but one with them."

In the sun-slanted Gothic office, over the green, opened Loeb
editions,
a splayed stack of geometric Greek,
my teacher said he felt he'd washed up on Nausicaä's island,
still agile, but wary, a relic from a more brutal age.

I said, "Mine would be a paper on the nature of the mystical
vision
in the *Agamemnon*. . ."
He looked out at me from the entrance into the House of
Atreus,
and said, "We all stand ankle deep in someone's blood."

". . . but with emphasis on Cassandra," I continued, "prisoner,
lover, oracle,
swept into a no-time in which all time is present,
a no-place everywhere at once, a vision fastened on the
moment of death,
which is the very nature of art."

"No," my teacher said, "her words are only what the wide,
                                        granite slabs
of the divine manage to press out of her."
I said, "But what she says is luminous, the essence of song."
"Sparrow," I called her,

"what the human mind could in duress become open to,
her own horrors notwithstanding. . . a lens of bright
                                        language. . .
the essence of poetry."
"One kind," he said, "and not mine".

ii.

He wanted poetry embedded in time,
in history, in earned truths of sequence,
that is to say, of syntax, slow and deliberate,
building the barrow stone by stone.
He craved too the base metal of irony,
its tacit image of a world in fracture.
Not the single vision, but signs of limits
on the human. A poetry of the day
after the peace has begun, when furies
have been talked back into the earth.
Not voices swept in with the whirlwind,
but those of the shelter, where whispered
kindnesses pass among those who survive,
who lie curled in the trunk of a hollow tree.

SEVEN TONGUES OF GOD

My first time, my friend said, nothing will change,
    everything will be the same, including myself,
       only more so.

I understood it to be what it is, an acid, an ergot derivative,
    a must, a blight on a rotten berry,
       a nausea in apparition,

but it feels like tripod molecules have landed on the moon,
    the cells applauding, while that marvel,
       the lacy architecture

of reason is melting to goose fat, to tendons and nerves
    with marrow-rich sockets of feeling
       which stretch out

like a sleek animal lodged under the skin. My heart is
    trotting like a tall horse under a tall rider,
       withers trembling

at the breeches and crop of aristocracy. The self I know
    has elided into the terrors of the dwarfed
       as it leaps the wall,

and crashes through leaves, stands stock-still, not
    even breathing. Shadows lick at
       its shoulders.

The cicadas sound like a cry for help, a plea for life,
    a life I have just begun to love,
       only more so.

BUBBLE NET

In a domain of pinion
and stridor, of blue heron,

and the cone of a mountain
gone crimson at sunset,

the herring at the surface
thrash, trapped in a ring

of bubbles, airy illusions,
while deep below a gaping

hungry humpback starts
to ascend. Who are you

to want what is less than
this, or other?

A Reading during Time of War

It is the moment just before,
        with no intent to punish,

a wish for all to be air
        and scrubbed by rain,

filled with eagerness to learn
        and be if not a child

then open-hearted, at ease,
        never to have heard

of the bending river
        that stretches to the delta

where a bloated corpse
        bumps softly,

snags on a tree stump
        and, waterlogged,

rolls slowly, just below.

FULL MOON BOAT

Yes, sell the compass, come on the boat of the full moon.
—Ho Chi Minh, "Full Moon in January," 1948

i. **Ensemble**

When the drumhead's skin is tightened
just enough, and the zither with inlaid
pearl discovers the key,

when the vibrato spool of the dan-bau
and the strings of the moon lute
find themselves,

when stick castanets and finger teacups
begin to shiver, and singers in carmine
silk begin their courting,

when a warm, steady rain starts to weep
over tiaras, and the back and forth
lean of planting,

then the northern lands will learn a river music,
and begin to flower.

ii. **The River Guard**

Tank-wallow,
moat of the mortared,
sap of cemeteries, their perfume bleeding
into waters steeped in sandalwood,

sweet vein of the Buddha we float on,
glistening pulse that scours the buffalo.
"This," says my friend leaning over the side,
". . . my Mother."

Of whom he lifts what he can, and drinks.

iii. **The Tea Stall**

We sit on worn, wobbly wooden stools.

Under a rusted corrugated roof,
heating in the midday sun
a pretty girl refills our cups.

She says she's not sure she'll ever marry,
and eyes the hired cars trying
to sneak onto the ferry,
the angry, red silk armband waving them back.

We look out on a farmer replanting
the rice-shoots one blade at a time.

You say that if it was up to you,
if poets could do long without cities,
or need other poets for more than tea or tobacco,

then you would live here in the flower forever.

iv. **The Kinh Thay Ferry**

We think they are crossing.
Here where bombs fell under the cries of the stork,
where dike walls are alive with winter grasses.
We think they are crossing again.

On the slope where the pavement ends
and willows are thin arms in the wind,
a woman squats by her bicycle,
a rice bale strapped to its rack, too heavy to push.

We think they are crossing here,
just beyond the lotus growing in the bomb-crater ponds,
just beyond the ferry's dented bow,
our arms pushing with her now.

Hué, in Darkness

at Nam Giao Altar

I think sometimes Hué is the centre of the universe,
that thousands of eyes have turned toward us here.
The reticent eye of the full moon with clouds.
The burning eye of the lit bundle of incense
wedged into stone.
The magnified eye of the imperial courtyard,
its marble sounding board.
The sceptical eye
of the woman praying on the shadowy steps.
The blinding eyes of the van's headlights.
And the soft pinpoints of candles cradled on the river.
The eyes of the many no longer here.
And the living eyes of friends who are.

ST. JOHN'S POINT
Donegal

After supper, we pedalled to a sandstone cove,
watched the tidepool dramas, the opal periwinkles,

waving sea lettuce, hermit crabs nibbling.
We wondered together what it might mean to depend

on the flat, warmed rocks slipping under the tide.
When we started back, it was pitch black everywhere,

and I asked if you'd ever heard of night vision,
how the iris will stretch to gather in ambient

light from stars, moon, and the distant city.
But there was none or little that night.

There was internment in the North, and imaginary
gunmen hiding in the ditches. A fine gravel

on the road made the wheels slip. On our faces
we could feel moisture from the ocean, hear

the thump of surf, and all the little mechanical
sounds of gear-teeth, sprockets, oily axles,

the squeak of saddle springs when we hit the ruts,
the metal of handlebars that sometimes touched.

FRAGMENTS ON THE LAST NIGHT

What would slip by stands
miraculously under the window,
hidden in a sentence, a phrase,
a ground fog lifting, or is it settling?

In a gravel wash, on a pale mossy
stalk of Great Mullein two goldfinches
grip, and the stalk sways like a wand.
It reminds me of breathing.

There are those who think the origin
of poetry is a deity. Others say it is
only a part of the self normally asleep.
Some will declare it is loss, that mortal

shale we all plummet toward.
Tonight I think it is more like breathing.
Like Whitman reciting poems
to the surf, aligning his rhythms,

like breathing. Like a day marked
by love for yourself and at least one
other, which is just like breathing,
only a little harder.

THE MEADOW

A friend spoke as if she thought I understood
something of her loss, and I pretended,
for reasons I cannot fathom, that I did,
and could say what would help her,
but that which came out
was kin to what we spit up after choking.

I said pain like this is a fire curtain we pass
through once and then we never feel quite
this way again. What I wanted to do
was open myself from sternum to throat,
pull out the organ of affection and learn
what it thought it had to teach.

In the meadow I see timbered logs,
the radiant centres of each, their knots,
their branches at the whorls. I see how
they bleed a silvery gum fragrant with age.

There is spring in the meadow, and it breeds
shapes which come and hover, round
ghostly presences, bleating sorry, very sorry.

That most innocent, indestructible of forms. . .

LEAN-TO

Into the dayroom long and polished as a bowling alley,
a nurse wheels in a tray with Dixie cups,
a few pills in each. The patients, none of them young,
and all women, are in varied states of psychosis
or stupor. Some are strapped at the wrist.
Others are belted at the chest to keep them upright.
An ebullient, grey-haired volunteer plays carols
and show tunes on a tiny harmonica.
"Who doesn't like music?" he asks us,
but my sister and I, we hardly notice.
The television is loudly on, the camera panning over
a banquet table, candles, the mound of the turkey,
a wainscot dining room. The camera cuts to another
part of the house where a lubricious interlude
has just finished. The actor is working at his Windsor knot
while she, in a slip, sits on the bed and brushes
her hair as if it were to blame.
(We grin. We sense we are going to like this part.)
He firmly declares, "I will not seek a divorce,"
and that his belief in family is unwavering,
despite what happened. She in the warm spirit
of the season says, "I understand, I knew what
I was getting into." Now it's back to the dining room
where someone murmurs "mouth-watering."
It is the moment the minister arrives.
We hope more illicit sex is in the offing,
and other forms of forgivable wickedness
we might have giggled over, years ago
when we sat together under a lean-to
we had made out of discarded Christmas trees.
It was then, while spruce needles fell on our hair,

she explained to me how male and female fit.
The sleet outside ticked so loudly on the icy sidewalk
we could hardly hear who was calling us in.
It was a voice which seemed as far away
from us as the nurse now blocking the TV,
who leans over and says, "It's your turn,
Mary Pat," and stays until she swallows.

NEW POEMS

AFTER THIS

There will be no more description,
no new moons with unnamed star
underneath, no implicit, reddening sun
on its way to see us again.

I will ask them all to hold back
awhile, to be more sceptical,
and see if we can appreciate
the uncertain, systemic balance,

the poise and capacity of being
to burn at such distances that
those eager to witness will declare
what they have seen is the light.

The rest of this, which is mostly dark
and descriptive, I have already erased.

AGAINST EPIPHANY

Which god was it that opened my picture
book and saw both of us on a road
where melting snowfields glittered
on every side and poplars bent like
the fingers of an old man clutching
at what he had loved about the sun?

Which one was it that saw behind
a thatched, white-washed farmhouse,
our fur, flies, and shit-stained walls?
And the barbed wire I had nailed
to fenceposts marking the boundary
of mind, and selfhood?

Which of the many stood gleaming
in sunlight, rime fringing the shore,
whitecaps like ice bobbing on the sea?
What was the nothing visible to whom
that god seemed to be waving?
What do we have that any god would want?

Quick, if you can find it, hide it.

THE CUSTODY OF THE EYES

Her eyes were green jewels,
not really jewels, but badly cut bottle-glass,
        and her skin was blushed up
with rouge, and as perfect as plastic allows.
        Her hair was hellish blonde
that is to say about to flame, or be ripped out
        of its almost visible sockets.
Around her neck a lace collar and a demi-choker
        of pearls. In the catacomb
cut at the centre of her chest (noting now it was
        deeper than her heart)
there was an opened kapok hand enshrined.
        Beneath her waist a swirl of plaster
moulding that served I think for pubic hair,
        but all outside her dress, made
thereby domestic as a low-slung apron.
        In between, inside her belly,
was a bronze photograph of five women.
        It had to have been a family,
their faces all wide-eyed, looking out through
        a central aperture of being,
ready to become as the mother seemed to know:
        someday nothing more than this.
The background if not the frame was a plain white
        dress splayed against the wall
like a paper cut-out, its hem made of chandelier
        spikes, as if all this might serve
as light for a ball. That is to say, there were no legs
        underneath, and there never was
a person here. Just her pursed, cupid lips;
        those cut, green eyes,
their stunned, wild, and empty staring.

FAMILY LIFE

hot sheep stink,
            delicious one-another.
to nuzzle against,
            yellowed, matted, oily

to stamp and huddle
            in the green hillside
through the sheets of rain,
            the crowning of clover

through radiant clusters
            of timothy, the child loves
her little, incipient life,
            most of it

Dear Lunacy

As if the moonlight could shift
the walls or melt them into
soggy cardboard, as if it could
bring the whole house down,
drag it over the blood-red cliff
and deliver us both.

As if it could be that much a friend,
and do more than light up
the cuts on her palm, rimmed with dirt.
Or show more than its weepy face
on the head of the nail I threaten
to drive in between my knuckles.

As if it could be more than what is
eaten while it grows. Or find its way out
of the burrow, that little cave where
she has taken herself away,
uneasy in her skin, knowing its value
on our particularly black market.

As if it could light up the way
to trap her, to talk her out of it,
to know more or better or to sing.
If only and all that, which holds nothing,
carries nothing compared to you,
handcuffed, cramped, and abundant you.

SPONGIFORM MAN

If at first I saw sea-fans waving in the current,
like wandering, wayward feelings,
then I had to assume the ocean floor was only venting,
and life had gathered round me there
as if I were the sulphured opening, the misted window in.

When I felt creation breathing through me,
there was only the pulse of direst need,
but now I was alone and witness to all I touched,
all that loved what I was and had become,
now at most a dark, greenly saddened

ground where I first fell as if praying,
as if an available, unwavering god would contain me,
a god who would confer more soul than this,
my trembling, unbowelled body.

CANTALOUPE DARLING

You have been compared to the finest
of God's human dimensions: firmer,
wanting more than mere licking.

Filled with bitter yellow seed,
your flesh as present and yielding
as August in the late-afternoon.

I remember the elegant spoon
my mother scraped you out with.
The carved, curved moon smiling.

I smell you now, weighing what
feels like immense consequence.
Bigger than my heart, and brain,

a skin as veiny as a lung, with
a corona at the base where you
were separated from the stem,

wounded, dying, and thus becoming
the simple body of pleasure,
an emblem of nothing deferred,

but of everything moist, easily
broken, and empty at the centre.
Alas, darling, I knew you well.

FRAGILE CONSTRUCTS OF MIND

Intersection where a girl died last year,
caution's blinking light as yellow as all
the early pansies that have sprouted up
in weathered, wooden bins, each so neat
that I do not know if I love life
enough to smile and admire, or hate it.

Or hate only those who are tuned so well,
are as certain of the future as their yards,
whose lives are already so neatly scoured
of branches and leaves that had blackened
under the snow, which place is where I
really want to go, back to, or in, or under.

I feel kinship perhaps with nothing but
prepositions, with dirt as the object,
the exception being a grey, feral cat
who limps by, whose lifespan in the wild
I have learned is three years at best.
I wish of course him nothing.

Diagnosis of Ibis

At this pond nothing
gathered anymore. . .
neither nesting eagle,
nor newt in mottle.

It was. It was
impossible and still
possible and. . .
what was wondrous

had all but fled;
her mind, her lovely mind
had found a long, white,
elegant feather,

and with each examined strand,
identical fear.

NIGHT HERON MAYBE

We woke to more rain, sheets of it,
and I felt in the dark for how wet
the sill had become. Then I rolled back
to the radio, its evangelical preacher
and his whisper of inevitable sin.
Lightning surprised the innocent shore,
and the thunder was a hollow sound
like that a bone will make breaking.

I do not know the names of birds by song,
and I do not know if this was the one
that sang, but out of the estuary
and the darkness, came a long, sleek,
and pointed call, as if this bird knew what
the given world gave and wanted more.

NOTE HELD

If it were nothing but sunlight,
or gleaming flashback over linoleum
flecked with flame, if it were only
a long corridor to the good little
hut of the self that curled onto
her mattress that was by design
only one inch high off the floor,
if it were not straps hung in curls
in the closet next to the bright room
with free cookies, cheese, crackers
in sealed packets, a fridge chocked
with icy juices, if it were not from
another locked room that we heard
a voice rising in anger, claiming she
too was or is a human being like you,
then I would not have answered
the questions they asked; I would
not have said I knew where I was
going, or where the building was,
or what unit, or that I understood
how day could lengthen into aching
spars of sunlight lined up over orderly
tulips and pansies. I would not, if I
could have helped it, let myself feel
nailed by one wrist to the desire to flee,
and by the other to a longing for sleep.
I would not have thought I knew what
a note feels like at the tips of gifted
fingers as they lift from the keys,
and allow tangible beauty to settle back
into what everyone says is ordinary pain.

THE SECRET

A digging fork, one tine bent
backward by a hidden, enormous stone.
In the wooden beams, ants,
with spiders feeding on their corpses.

Filaments in air,
tightropes they've walked on before.

A cement floor lifted
by roots slowly breaking in.

My father's narrow desk,
the one his bills bled him over.

My fingers cold, just this side of aching.
Folding doors wide-open.

Nothing more.

PART OF IT

for Faraj Sarkohi

When I started home, a woman was lost
at the platform edge saying something
no-one could understand, and on the train
a middle-aged father was whispering

with his eyes across the aisle to his son.
There are certainly more words for god
than snow, and there are flags that flicker
in the slightest wind, but my own words

were lost then in the way you spoke
of the many confessions you had made,
made happily. Torture, you said, was
a doorway, and the hanging lasted only

until you blacked out. When you woke,
assuming that had been the end,
you felt sharp disappointment
the afterlife should look so familiar.

Today in this world, the warmest day
of the year so far, I look out and see
the maple leaves have unfolded
into yellow-greens that will for a while

feel as soft as the flesh of an infant,
and for a little while longer will
whisper as if they too assume all
they are saying is what we can hear.

THE SUNFLOWER
for William Stafford

It must have been something charming
that the poet has said,
for all three of us are laughing,
but he has the gleam of the imp,
as if he knew one secret of longevity
was some form of decency.
I would bet you he has told a story,
something about a child who has fallen
in love for life with a library.
Or the way a classroom
has become refuge and doorway,
and ink on the fingers
has turned into treasure even a mother
cannot wash off.
Or it could have been
more about himself growing old,
the way certain books will travel
well, share your bed, never want
to leave you in the morning.
Or maybe something harder to pin down,
a thought that swayed in his mind
like summer grasses. A thought
that had to be whispered.
He has bowed his head deliberately
in order to tell us. It is as if
he is leaning over a fence,
to say something memorable,
but, as I said, we are laughing,
as if listening to him tell a joke.

FIRST SONG AGAIN

Trust all the wood you stand on,
Become an ally of the grain.
Bend in the wind.

Trust even the high, precarious places,
The steeples and windy overhangs
That teach you everything.

Trust too the rose-tint of late afternoon
Sifting down through a lofted
Blue heron wing.

And trust above all the imminent return
Of the small, but persistent
Impulse to sing.

BODEGA BAY, 1969

for Edwin Honig

We left unwashed the chipped plates
with maple syrup warming
out in the bigger sun of the West.
We walked and must have talked,
but all I remember is
the near silence of the pale yellow
grasses sawing at our legs, barbed
wire at the boundary,
a salt lick, a spigot and a trough.
We must have talked about your war,
you in Germany at the end,
translating near the camps, and not the war
I believed I was destined for, a sent
witness to the emptiness
and my idea of the poet's absolved,
absolving identity. We must have
poked around like bees
that day at the edge of a transparency,
our feelers at the window of immanence,
its glass sheeting of death,
hoping we could find one of the ways out.

WAR STORY

Since we are of the species
claiming a soul different from
the animals, it is no surprise
that today my first undeliberate
thought when I woke was of
how easy it would be to call in
artillery, to walk it slowly across
the fields of the past, the horses
grazing there, the children with
books, the soaking clothes that
hang and dry, to bring it home
and do this without thinking,
to take vague pride in what
I honestly know is achievement,
though it is to think like a horse
who early in life had been trained
to move around an oily spindle
and think he gets somewhere.

MESCALINE STORY

She felt the visionary promise
of the mauve tablets I pulled
out and placed on the table.
Right away, she declared we
must fly to the Casa de Campo,
to watch the horses out for their
morning canter, the riders in their
exquisite twill, fawn, and velvet.

When we got there, the cedars
in the distance bowed like servants.
Horses strapped in gleaming leather
nodded at us as if they knew we had
joined them in the experience of
the body. The feeling that flickered
across the spring meadow was filled
with purple and yellow wildflowers,

and we were scented by the grasses
that warmed to our neighing and
nuzzling each other with such love
we could hardly imagine the bit,
that cold and joined angle of iron
we were pretending to spit.

MEDICINE

Eight, and we were under the porch.
It may have been doctor,

but I remember it was imaginary war-time
that had her tending wounded me.

How that evolved into our clothes coming off
I don't really know. Perhaps an appeal

to her sense of fairness had met with a bright,
midmorning, summertime curiosity

slanting through in rows of narrow stripes
across the little secrets where

we could see the first dust of years,
a soft grey talc of stillness and neglect.

And where it began to settle,
that was where we touched.

FELL OF DARK

When you learn to thank whatever
you can believe in for snow,
for the water that drips off the gutter,
for the small hole in the snow
where it bled (more water than light,
more ice melting, more than air can hold)
when you sweep snow off the window
designated yours, and beat your gloves
against the chest before you key open
the wreathed door and step in,
when you stamp this that clings to your boot,
as if it were just light and lovely sorrow,
then you know, or pretend to know
these precious gifts that bring you in.

BIG DIG DREAM

Bookshelves have been pushed
to the wall. We enter into a sea
of red carpet, but no one wears
makeup. It is still daylight.

Each of us bears recent losses
as we listen to singing which is
timed unwittingly to workers outside
wielding in a ditch their pickaxes.

I have walked near many such digs,
have looked long at young men labouring,
hemmed in by what would pass
for anyone as a terrible given.

Because I have looked down upon them,
even in kinship, I am certain I will
be punished for something I have forgotten,
and on which another's life depends.

Now I am swinging at the earthen wall
desperate to uncover what I have done
to deserve this. When awareness
comes to me it is without a name.

The recognition comes to me
the way music does when it first touches
the elbow, and you turn slowly
toward someone you never dreamed was there.

Or, it is as if one of your own hands
has reached down, and your other hand
has reached up to grasp it.
The light around them both is pure blue.

HOUSE ON WATER, HOUSE IN AIR

These places kept, where we keep
and where we can't, the river.
Where the riverbank is firm,
but crumbling, where the slate
of long ages shows bones dissolving.

Along these a boy among the living thinks
that nothing is near, or worth believing in.
That every bit of air comes from where
he will never get and the house lifted from
its mooring feels like his soul in longing.

While in the room remain traces
of the adult, the underwear scattered,
brown drops of blood, a corpse set loose,
rolling on the floor, in this house made of air,
this house nailed by less than dream.

House that drifts with the flood of all
he thought he wanted, house that floats
on a muddy river in spring-time flood,
house like a human head on the surface,
house with a boy's face, turned up.

Poems from the Vietnamese

OCCASIONAL VERSES AT CON SON, AFTER THE WAR

by Nguyen Trai (1380-1422)
co-translated with Nguyen Ba Chung

Ten years away from what I knew and loved as home,
I return to pine and chrysanthemum grown rampant,
to patient streams and trees wondering where I've been.

I am covered in dust.
There was nothing else I could do.

Now that I am home, my life seems nothing but a dream.
The war may be over, I may be alive, but I want nothing
more than a cloud-tipped mountain, good tea, a stone pillow.

RICE FROM OUR VILLAGE

by Tran Dang Khoa
co-translated with Nguyen Ba Chung

Rice from our village
holds the flavours of the rich
dark silt from the Kinh Tay,
and the lotus growing in the spill pond.
It holds the bitter-sweet notes
of my mother's songs.

Rice from our village
survived the storms of July,
and the downpours of March.
It has soaked up our sweat
in sweltering, mid-day June,
when the paddy is so hot
even the fish cannot breathe,
and crabs scuttle out the water
in search of shade. That is
when my mother wades in,
and bends to set the seedlings.

Rice from our village
has survived bombs made in America
and aimed at our rooftops.
It has trudged to the front with our soldiers
and their rifles, our rice,
with its stalks and grain-heavy heads
yellow as the brass of bullets.
All through the soldiers' trenches
the sweet smell of our rice.

Rice from our village
has struggled through the long droughts,
laboured with the children
as they lifted water from paddy to paddy
in worn-out bamboo buckets,
trolling for plant-hungry worms,
the children no taller than the rice stalks
that scraped their faces
as they lugged those buckets
just barely off the ground.

Rice from our village
has travelled to the front, and far beyond.
Oh let me sing praises for this,
the rice from our village,
this gold. . .

THE LAND BEYOND THE CITY

by Nguyen Khoa Diem
co-translated with Nguyen Ba Chung

In the land beyond the boundaries of the city,
the wash is scattered along the riverbanks.
The poor are gathered there too, like heaps
of shellfish dumped on a pier in the afternoon.

In the land beyond the boundaries of the city,
the people hurry to and fro, Early Market
and Late, dawn to dusk, the feet bare, the shirts
tattered, and backs breaking under heavy sun.

I grew up in one of those houses
in the sad land beyond the city,
where old, wandering Mr. Trau
no longer sings, where the palaces
are hidden behind thick forest,
their doors locked. The young
in their white shirts no longer sit
in those ancient gardens reading
poems while outside on the streets
busy people scuffed past. Now
it's only cyclo drivers sipping drinks
in the afternoon, under the wavering
shade of a rusting roof. Only a heavy heat
pounding on the flimsy stalls that cling
to the roadside. Only my mother,
selling souvenirs all through the rains,
her grief for her lost husband stubborn
and cold as the rain on her glass cases.

Only these lives falling apart slowly,
the way the road at Dap Da crumbles
in the annual flood.

What was it I felt the most —
the fire of *phuong*-tree leaves,
or the flames in my heart —
when we left behind that sad row of houses?
Fifteen long years ago, not days.
Time enough for a childhood friend
to become a man who knows war.

But there has never been a spring morning
like this one. We seem to fly above the line
of fire, as even the earth itself seems to rise up
against our enemy to chase after their heels.
Mang Ca fortress has been shattered,
Phu Bai base shredded.

In the land beyond the boundaries of the city
now a hundred doors open for us.
Our rockets are armed with our own blood.
O, mothers, sisters, comrades who watch
from the old houses with tear-filled eyes,
we have come into ourselves, into our own being.
Our century of yearning now claims the streets.
The land beyond the boundaries of the city
has become the rampart of our fortress,
the Perfume River the centre.

My mother, I am glad to have been born here
and grateful for all you have given me, through sun

and rain, for that is what I have held onto
through fifteen years of searching.

Now in an arc of tracers, and at long last
I salute my father too. I return to stand
at our altar in front of his photograph,
the old man who had fought the French.
It has taken me all these years to see him again.
As my friends light the joss sticks, the incense
rises, and my father's eyes seem to brighten,
as if he floated now in the sea of our new flag.

In the land beyond the boundaries of the city
the songs rise and the heart pounds with pride.
Now we have taken back the port at Thuan An.

1/1968 - 4/1969